TABLE OF CONTENTS

"The interval between the decay of the old and the formation and the establishment of the new, constitutes a period of transition which must always necessarily be one of uncertainty, confusion, error, and wild and fierce fanaticism."
- John C. Calhoun, American Senator

I dedicate this book:

To my boys, Matthew and Michael, who are now successful young men traveling their own confident paths and exploring life's many happy treasures. I am so very proud of you both. Giving life to you will always be my greatest accomplishment. I love you more than life itself.

To Brian, the father of my boys. Although our journey changed and we have taken different paths, I will always love you for who you are. You wrapped me unconditionally in your wings and set me free when the time was right. You will always have a piece of my heart.

To my husband, Nick, who inspires me every day to be a better person. Your unconditional, uncompromising, never-ending love gives me the courage I need to take one more step even though I could fall off the edge. With your support, I have found the sheer excitement of not knowing but still embracing what is. You are my anchor. xo

INTRODUCTION:

Are you the woman who has looked at herself in the mirror and shuddered at what she saw? The one who lives life out of obligation and with resignation? Are you that woman who has given up because society says you don't fit? Are you that woman who says I'm just too damn tired to _____? If you are, then this book is dedicated to you.

With this book, however, comes a timeout.

Go to your room, lock the door and re-learn your life. I want you to reflect on what you've done, on what you've created and most importantly, what foundation you've built your life on. It's common sense to take an umbrella if it's raining outside. Likewise, if it's snowing you wear your boots and if it's hot you wear shorts. Similarly, your common sense must spill over into your thoughts. If your thoughts aren't in alignment with your values and purpose, change them. It's time to feel a little uncomfortable, to release people and things that no longer fit you, literally and figuratively.

I am encouraging you to say goodbye forever to the conditioned beliefs that we as women have been taught; whether about your body or your role in life. I am here to tell you that you can relearn in a kinder, gentler way.

I am here to proclaim that this is the decade of deliciously double-sized divas – bigger thoughts, bigger confidence and most importantly, a bigger understanding of who you really are at a soul level. If it doesn't fit, throw it out; if doesn't make you happy, re-think it; and most of all, if it doesn't support your greatest and highest good, re-invent it.

Throughout this book I will reveal my personal experiences in a way that provides learning and awareness. My intention is to empower all who read this to become curious about themselves. My words are intended to inspire each reader to have a relationship with her Soul.

I have created this book/journal for you to share your most intimate thoughts and feelings. It's a nurturing environment where your Soul can grow. As you read my words, absorb the energy of the love I have placed behind them. Know that you are never truly alone. Every path you have walked or will walk, we have all done so at one time or another.

Throughout this book you will see pieces of me revealed. I will write from the perspective of the emotionally scarred little girl, the mean, evil, manipulative adulteress, and the mature spiritually-centered teacher.

My wish is that this book will guide you to the realization that acceptance is where it all begins. Yes, acceptance of what IS. Love what IS right now. Free yourself of judgment and self-defeating thoughts. Empower yourself with reflections of who your Creator made you to be, and embrace the unshakable courage that comes from being who you are right now.

CHAPTER 1

Screaming
on the Inside

For me, 1984 was the year of pasta. I remember it as if it were yesterday. I was a young stay- at-home mom who loved her baby boy more than life itself. We'd play together, nap together, eat together and cry together. It is only in hindsight that I can see exactly how depressed I was. It is also hindsight that brings me to the conclusion that I wasn't suffering the famous post-partum depression, but rather an inherited form of the disease.

From all perspectives, life was great. My baby was finally healthy after a long, arduous battle to heal him from a rare disease. I was a 22-year-old homeowner, mother, and wife. I had what I always dreamed of as a child: a happy, loving family. So, why was I drowning myself in food?

My idea of a happy afternoon was to put my son down for a nap, and boil a POUND of elbow macaroni, stir in a can of tomato sauce, and gorge myself while watching soap operas. This pattern continued until my second son was born three years later. For me, it was more than just eating; most times I wasn't even hungry. It was a comfort, a familiar pattern I had adopted as a child to insulate me from the tumultuous life of an alcoholic father, mentally ill mother, and sickly brother. When I was in the eye of the storm, I saw nothing except a beautiful, happy, fluffy me. I was "safe" in that world.

After the birth of my second son, I sank deeper into depression. I felt worthless, and my eating habits continued to spiral out of control. My weight had ballooned to more than 230 pounds. I was so miserable on the inside, but still pretending to be happy on the outside. I was the life of the party; always the first to make you laugh. I was the person everyone gravitated toward, because I still displayed a façade of happiness.

In 1988, my son was graduating from pre-school. I'd purchased a new outfit, got a new hairstyle and was ready to show it all off. What I wasn't ready for were the pictures I saw the following day. You see, I had gotten very good at never being in photos (too much reality for me). Even though the photos taken by my husband showed me approaching the stage to congratulate and embrace my son, all I could focus on was how huge I looked. For the first time, I realized the physical effects of my love/hate relationship with food. The week that followed is still a blur, but I know it involved lots of eating.

After days of sitting and clutching the dreadful picture in one hand and a bag of peanut M&M's in the other hand, I made the decision to go to Weight Watchers. Unbeknownst to me, this would be yet another attempt to shed the misery of my past.

Fast forward nine months: success! I had lost 68 pounds. I had NEVER been so thin in my life. I was a whole new person, physically and emotionally. What I didn't realize was that this new person I had become lacked substantial moral character and was still an adult-in- progress. With my newfound freedom, I would find another way to self-sabotage. I'll share more about that later.

WHAT SOCIETY TELLS US
If you look a certain way you will feel a certain way…

The female body has been admired from the beginning of time. However, criticism of the female body has never been more prevalent than it is today. Full-figured women are in; svelte sickly thin women are in. Curvy busty women are in. What exactly does "in" mean, and who defines it? Fashion magazines, Hollywood producers, or the average guy on the street? And, if you are not

"in", what does that imply? Must you sneak out only at night? Wear a bag over your head in daylight?

I've concluded that it's not your genes, but rather, your jeans that we are told "make" us. Skinny, low-rise, cropped, fitted, spandex-infused, adorned with a designer label, and cut four sizes too small!

And let's not forget Spanx. Or those paper-thin models in size zero jeans who entice us to eat their favorite cereal for two weeks so we can look like them. It's no wonder we end up wallowing in a pool of pasta when we are constantly bombarded by messages telling us we're not good enough. Add our conditioned beliefs to Madison Avenue advertisers' messages about the ideal beauty, and we are headed straight for disastrous relationships with ourselves.

For example, consider the woman in the commercial who has a horrible day, only to get home and show us that, like her, we can banish our blues if we simply eat the brand of cheese she's promoting. As a real woman, I'd prefer a heaping plate of pasta and some wine to a tiny triangle of cheese. But alas, the voice in my head returns: "You're too chubby, your face is too round, and your clothes are size 16. You shouldn't eat pasta." Pulled back to harsh realities, I count my points, attend Jenny program meetings, eat only protein-rich foods, or show the ultimate level of commitment: sitting patiently by my front door, salivating while waiting for the UPS delivery guy to bring my pre-ordered, pre-cooked, pre-portioned, "nutritious" week's supply of slimming food. And I am internally tortured by multiple thoughts of failure.

THE TIMES WE LIVE IN!
The gimmicky 100-calorie snack packs and the low-fat/no-fat head games get more ridiculous by the day. Last night I sat down

ready to enjoy one of those 100-calorie bags of popped kettle corn. I put it in the microwave for a minute or so, and poured my glass of wine (which, naturally, exceeded the two-ounce limit). The microwave beeped, my snack was done and so was I with the entire bag two minutes later. Of course it has only 100 calories; there are only ten kernels to be popped in the bag. It finally occurred to me that we are paying for portion control while companies charge double the price for half the product. Is it our need to fit in that overrides our common sense?

And don't forget the over-indulgent voices in our heads, voices that relentlessly remind us we aren't good enough until we _____. You know that voice; your arch nemesis. It makes us want to hide, forbids us to wear a bathing suit, bans us from giving and shames us into cancelling dinner and social plans. It's the voice that we pacify with a cookie or a bag of potato chips.

After a lot of hard work, I had become a mirror image of the accepted women seen on the pages of beauty magazines, yet I was still miserable. In fact, after losing all the weight my life got worse. Advertisers want us to believe that if we look a certain way, life will be easier. What they neglect to tell us is that this is untrue.

I was determined to find a way to silence that voice inside of me that told me I wasn't good enough, smart enough, or pretty enough. After years of experimenting I have concluded that there is only one way to soothe that distressing voice: connecting to my Soul. I believe the Soul is a direct connection to our Creator. It is the place within where the Divine resides.

You're probably wondering how we begin to transform into beings that live life from our soul. It begins with living a conscious life, which means having an awareness of one's environment and one's own existence, sensations, and thoughts. In other words, it's about being mindful of who we are and what we are here to do.

Living consciously involves keen awareness. You are already thinking, and in order to live consciously, all you have to do is to be aware of what you are thinking. This takes sincere effort. I have the attention span of an ant, but with practice I now am able to choose which thoughts to focus on in regards to my body and my life.

I routinely check in with my soul; that place in the center of my being that is like a built-in barometer for life. By checking in regularly you can begin to recognize what the sensations mean. For example, has the hair on the back of your neck ever stood on end upon meeting someone for the first time, but rather than following your gut reaction to walk away, you got involved anyway, only to find it wasn't in your best interest to do so? Inevitably we say, "I should have listened to my gut." When you become the expert of listening to your Soul, you quickly learn to walk away to avoid chaos. Your internal knowing will never let you down. Your job is to connect and tune in. When you are living consciously, you will follow that feeling back to your core, your gut, your Soul and save yourself a lot of angst. Learn to trust your feelings. The underlying issue here is trust. Trust yourself, and trust the fact that no one can ever have YOUR answers. You are the only one who has your answers. Search within for a response. Why would you trust anyone else to answer for you?

Once you become conscious, life becomes sweeter, easier, and more manageable. I am not saying that it's problem-free or stress-free, but manageable in a completely different way.

Reflection
What am I willing to trust today?

What have I been doing to sabotage trust in myself?

What intentions can I put forward to build trust in myself?

Quietly ponder your intentions every day for the week. Practice listening to your inner voice. Sit quietly and let spirit, God, Universe, Divine guide you.

How might fear stop me from trusting myself? Fear blocks you from trusting your intuition. List all your fears surrounding your intention.

What would help my body feel loved this week? Get quiet and ask your body what it needs from you. What kind of self-talk – that little voice in your head that tells you everything from you're not good enough to you're perfect just as you are, and everything in between – have I been using lately? Am I kind and loving to myself or am I critical and demanding? Explore your self-talk with words.

Today I am grateful for…

JOURNAL

CHAPTER 2

Soulology:
The Study of the Soul

Soul *(n) 1: The immaterial essence, animating principle, or actuating cause of an individual life. 2: The spiritual principle embodied in human beings, all rational and spiritual beings, or the universe. 3: A person's total self.*
– Merriam-Webster online dictionary

What is the Soul?

The Soul is where the Divine dances with the human. It's our connection to the Creator; I say it IS where the Creator lives in us. Imagine a place where there is no judgment, a place where there is only acceptance and love, a place where all intentions and thoughts are pure. That's where our Soul resides. As you read the passage below, allow yourself to be transported to a place that is beautiful, warm and meaningful: your Soul.

Today I am blessed to have my physical surroundings include a glass of sparkling water with lime on the table beside me. To my left, a crystal blue ocean with shining stars on its wave crests, and to my right, a gently rippling, white curtain that conceals the luminous surface of a swimming pool. Ceiling fans and bamboo umbrellas swaying in the cool ocean breeze complete the most peaceful feeling I've ever had.

In the non-physical realm, I am faced with thoughts of my true existence. My personal truth is that everything I need is already within my reach, and all I have to do is turn up the awareness. I am reminded once again that I do not need to be transported anywhere for the answers. All I need to do is simply look within. However, that realization sure does come easier when I am peering into one of God's greatest creations.

Like the ocean, our Souls are deep and full of unknown treasures if only we are open to going deep enough to discover them. Just as we must approach the ocean with a high level of respect and reverence, we must also honor our Souls. The Soul is the place where there is no hiding, no pretending, no conning and no room for falsehoods. The depth of the Soul is where the source of all life resides. The depth of our being is the only place where we can go that is truly safe and sacred. It's the place where we are unconditionally loved with limitless patience and tolerance, and the place we are accepted for who we are, not for what we have.

Too often we fall short, blindly dive within and we are left feeling emptier than when we began the exploration. Could it be that we are blinded by our expectations and worldly views? I propose we look within with an open mind and reverence to explore every fiber of ourselves, not just the parts that we like or the parts that society accepts or people compliment us on. We must also consider the parts that are hidden beneath the rubble of our past.

It is helpful to cleanse the Soul and purge that which no longer serves us. This is the only way to experience inner peace and self-acceptance. Inner peace brings a priceless sense of self-assured calmness. We know everything is just as it should be. We must release our need to control situations and embrace flexibility to become like the palm tree that bends but doesn't break in a hurricane. Dive into your deepest treasures.

If just for today, I encourage you to go into the ocean of your Soul and search for the buried treasure of Self. This treasure hunt promises rewards and pleasant surprises all along the journey. Go ahead and embrace your Soulful Mystery with all its undiscovered gifts. Breathe in slowly and observe your thoughts about what's in your Soul.

Reflection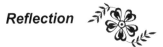

What am I most passionate about this week?

_____

What attracts my attention?

_____

What does my Soul desire this week?

_____

What do I want to say "no" to this week?

_____

What is it that will drain my energy if I do not set boundaries and practice saying no?

_____

_____

What do I want to give myself permission to do to honor who I am at a Soul level? What makes me feel joy?

_____

_____

What nurtures and calms my Soul? *Is it a walk in the rain or curling up with a great book and cup of tea for a snuggle with a pet? Explore your Soul.*

_____

_____

Today I am grateful for...

_____

_____

JOURNAL

CHAPTER 3

THINKING

Have you ever had a day when everything seemed to go your way from the start? The sun was shining, it was a "good hair day," and every traffic light you approached remained green. Perhaps you got a surprise phone call, or experienced a day with no bills in the mailbox.

On the flip side, how about the day when you stubbed your toe stumbling out of bed, you ran out of hot water mid-shower, or even spilled coffee on your blouse? Those days always seem to turn out very differently, don't they? In fact, we often find ourselves calling it "one of those days."

Once the tone of the day is set – good or bad – we seem to allow it to continue on its path. But days can turn into weeks, into years and ultimately into the rest of your life. What tone are you setting in your life?

The amazing thing is that you have the power to change it. Just like Dorothy learned when she returned from Oz, you have had the power to change your life all along.

Physicists now know that thought, as neural impulse, is energy. All energy follows the same principle. As the saying goes, "like attracts like." So, we attract what we think about. Changing your circumstances actually begins with a very simple yet very profound act: changing your thoughts.

The concept of "mind over matter" is not new. We've heard many stories of miraculous healing and ordinary people overcoming extraordinary physical limitations. With recent scientific advances, we can now chart the pathways of our thoughts down to the genes within each cell. According to the latest medical breakthrough, it

has been revealed that paying attention to our thoughts allows us to change what were once believed to be our pre-destined conditions. If you follow a thought on its journey, it will take you first through the brain and then into the body, and then all the way down to the genes themselves.

In a recent interview, Dr. Candice Pert, an internationally recognized pharmacologist, described the interface or junction where thoughts affect us physically, stating, "Emotions are the currency of exchange between our mind and body."

Hence, if your emotions are vibrating at a low level (negative or stressful thoughts), they could manifest as physical disease. Decay or disease of your body can indeed start as a toxic thought. These days, we tend to have more toxic thoughts as our stress levels rise. What will you think yourself into? It's time to free yourself from this disease-thought trap.

Meet Sally. What Was She Thinking?

It is important to understand that our thoughts create the life we have, and that most of the time, we think in "autopilot mode." We rely on our conditioned beliefs that are handed down from our family to guide us through life. I'd like to introduce you to "Sally." It is plain to see that "Sally" is telling me who she is, using her old beliefs.

At a recent event where I was being introduced to various women in the community as a Relationship Coach, women gazed at me curiously and wondered what to think about me. One woman who was quite forward bounced into my space and proceeded to introduce herself to me. It went something like this, "Hi, I'm Sally, the Mayor of such and such, you know the one who embezzled money from the town. " After that introduction I was mesmerized by her. Her gregarious, seemingly confident approach soon dwindled. She had a few words to share with me about her life including the charges and how she paid her dues. Toward the end of our conversation she asked me a question that I found very simple to answer.

"Can you give me some pointers on how to find the right man?" she asked.

"You can begin with losing the introduction you used on me," I replied, without missing a beat.

We shared a chuckle, but interestingly enough I saw a spark inside of her. We proceeded to share some time reflecting on her story; the very story she was using in all her relationships and potential relationships. The energy behind the words is one of I'm not good enough, I'm a loser, I will always be guilty and I will always wear my guilt for the entire world to see. She was continually reminding herself and the world that she wasn't worthy. Therefore, that is what she was attracting. Very easy for me to see and I'm sure very easy for you the reader to identify. We cannot see our own stories as clearly as we see others.
If it is true – and I do believe it is— that our thoughts can make us sick, how do we re-learn what we have already adopted as truth? Awareness! Create your awareness.

I'd like to suggest you take a moment and think back to the last time you met someone new; someone who you've never seen before, someone who knows nothing about you. What was your opening line? What was your follow-up conversation like? What were you feeling at that moment? A moment is all we have sometimes to define how we will be seen. What are you projecting?

Reflection

What thoughts am I willing to throw out?

_____

How can I grow from past mistakes and weaknesses made by old thoughts?

_____

Am I willing to plant the seeds of a new beginning?

_____

If you are struggling to identify mistakes or weaknesses, draw a line down the center of a paper and list weaknesses and mistakes on one side, and potential growth from those same weaknesses and mistakes on the other.

What is my biggest source of stress this week? What are my thoughts around the stress? How can I shift perspective and create a manageable thought process?

_____

_____

What story rumbling around in my thoughts am I telling myself about that stress? Get quiet and talk openly and honestly with yourself. Take a pencil and paper and let it flow freely from you. Purge it all.

_____

_____

What are the facts about my stress?

_____

_____

Today I am grateful for...

_____

_____

_____

_____

_____

JOURNAL

CHAPTER 4

Making Your Thoughts Work for You

~ The Law of Attraction

Constant negativity will fill your life with worry, angst and tension. It will cause your life-force to vibrate at a lower frequency, thus creating disease. However, if you feed yourself positive thoughts filled with love, tolerance and acceptance, your life will always be full of joy and happiness with blessings of good health and fortune because positive thoughts and actions compel the Divine Spirit to help and protect you.

The Law of Attraction is about consistently focusing on and thinking positive emotions that will move you forward in life. ***Disclaimer*** *The Law does not differentiate between good and bad emotions. If you want something badly and feel very positive about it, you will most likely get it. On the other hand, if you do not want something and feel negatively about the prospect of having it, then you will probably get it, too.*

Everything around us vibrates; every piece of existence is a form of electromagnetic energy. We, as humans, are made up of energy. Every MRI or EKG procedure you've ever had shows your internal energy map.

Everything in the universe is made up of atoms and every atom in the universe is made of subatomic particles. Every subatomic particle is made up of energy or light which can be subdivided into particles or waves. These particles or waves are flashing constantly in and out of existence millions of times a second. Imagine lights being switched off and on, or the flashing of a strobe light. Essentially, the entire universe is flashing continuously. We do not see it, but our Souls and subconscious minds are always tuned in.

Your every thought interacts with the energy of the universe. Negative thoughts hook up with other negative thought energies because their matching vibrating frequencies connect them. Negative energy vibrates at a lower frequency because it is denser and heavier. An environment of negative thought energy is created and forms a thought wave. These powerful negative thought waves manifest themselves in our lives in the form of poverty and crime.

Negative energy detracts from the life-giving nature of the universe. You recognize the labels we give to negative thoughts as bad luck, misfortune, disaster and evil. The source of all of this resides within us. Remember, what you think about is truly what matters.

On the upside, positive thought energy also seeks out other positive energies. If you are a source of positive thought energy, positive and beneficial energy will return to you in many wonderful ways. Everything that happens in your life connects directly to the type of energy with which you are charging the universe. Positive energy vibrates at a higher frequency because it is finer and lighter. Think about what it feels like to be happy or in love. You're light and airy, almost buoyant. You alone are responsible for the type of energy created by your life.

What Was I Committed to Creating?

Back to the post- weight loss me; circa 1990. We had recently purchased our second home; it was a typical scene of suburbia;

a serene, tree-lined street where kids rode bikes and played baseball. I was almost 70 pounds lighter and living "the dream". My husband had a very secure career and I was beginning a new career myself. We drove new cars, enjoyed wonderful family vacations, and renovated our home, yet I still ached. I couldn't seem to find the place inside of me where the ache emanated from. I liken it to having an itch and not quite knowing where exactly to scratch. All the "right" things were appearing for me. Why wasn't I happy? What more did I need? Apparently, I needed chaos, destruction and pain because that is what I gave myself throughout the 1990s.

It is very apparent to me that we attract to us what and who we are. In the early 90's I had an extramarital affair. I willingly and knowingly cheated on my husband, but more importantly than that I cheated myself out of respect, and love. I entered into this horrific affair with a man 17 years my senior. He was an alcoholic, a narcissist, and he worshipped me in a way that I knew. Having come from a background that included an alcoholic parent and a mentally ill parent I had learned that love was supposed to hurt. It was how I had always identified love, if you don't hurt me how will I know you love me? My husband was too good. I was suspicious of him. How could he expect me to believe that he loved me when he wasn't physically or emotionally abusive or abandoning me. How dare he profess his love for me. The "other man", I knew him my entire life, figuratively. He mentally and physically abused me and that was a feeling I was OK with. It was a safe feeling for me.

When I say that we attract to us who we are, I know it firsthand. The "other man" was a reflection of exactly who I was in that moment in time; a scared, insecure coward who had no regard for anyone else. Little by little as I kept going to therapy and kept searching within, I began to pull myself up and away from the hell that was the 90s. A lot of the tools I used to find my way home to my Soul are spread throughout this book. I can't attribute any one process to the healing that occurred but I can say with complete conviction it included a radical acceptance of what IS, a strong will to change what was, a creative vision of what I wanted my life to be, many pitfalls and finally God.

Reflection

When was the last time you lovingly embraced your wholeness just as you are? I want to help you to create better Self-awareness. Remember I said earlier if you are aware, you are conscious. Moreover, if you are conscious, you can choose the path that supports your highest and greatest good. Before you begin this Self-awareness journey, you should ask yourself: "Am I willing?" Commit now: I have willingness to

_____

_____

What do I want in my life?

_____

_____

Am I willing to take a small, sweet step toward what I want?

_____

List what you are willing to do to get closer to what you want:

_____

A conditioned thought is one we learned growing up either from our immediate family or from surroundings in general. List how your conditioned thoughts are limiting you:

_____

_____

_____

_____

Am I willing to come out of my conditioned thoughts about _____?

What am I feeling at this moment in my life?

_____

_____

I have always wanted to _____, and I am willing to do this to make it happen:

_____

JOURNAL

CHAPTER 5

Transforming Yourself

For the Better

Change can only happen is you are aware and if you are willing. In order to transform ourselves we must first set our sights on what we intend our lives to "look" like. The process to begin the transformation contains the following ingredients:

Insight: Plant a seed of Insight. Begin with a thought.

Timing: Timing really is everything. Know yourself; know your timing. Get quiet. Develop excellent timing through silence. While sitting in stillness, listen for the voice of God within. Trust the messages coming through.

Patience: Don't rush Divine order. Know when to bloom; feel it in your Soul. Trust your intuition.

Surrender: Let go of your story. Let go of the need to control. Spiritually surrender to a Higher Power.

Grounding: If a tree has deep roots, it is stronger. The same is true for you. Immerse yourself in something bigger than yourself. Everyone with whom we come into contact is our teacher. All we have to do is realize this for the learning to take place.

Growth: When given the correct amount of what it needs, a flower will thrive. Similarly, when you **nurture your thoughts, they, too, will bloom abundantly.** Your evolution will be as natural and organic a process as the grass growing and the sun rising.

Transformation: The seeds of your insight will take root, and you will glow with the joy of traveling the highest path.

This transformation will be your direct connection to knowing. If this is something you have been striving for, I am here to tell you that you already possess the knowing. In order for you to strengthen or to recognize that connection, you must first quiet your mind. Spirit is always with you and always willing to talk to you. Are you always willing to listen?

Transformation Exercise

To begin the exercise, sit comfortably. Do a few neck rolls to loosen your shoulders and release tension. Allow your mind to wander anywhere it wants to go. As your mind wanders, take notice of where it is going and gently call it back to the present. Count to four as you inhale deeply through your nose.

Focus on the inhale. Feel how great it feels to fill your lungs. Hold the breath to the count of seven. Release by exhaling deeply through your mouth with a whoosh (pucker your lips if necessary to make the sound). Count to eight as you expel the breath. As this becomes rhythmic and soothing, consciously ask questions and open your mind to whatever flows in. This consciousness is all that is needed to communicate with Spirit. Spirit resides in the conscious mind.

Practice a daily routine of getting quiet. Never place any pressure on yourself. Simply allow the process to happen when the time is right. Remember that Self-development is an individual process and no two people experience it in the same way. The journey is as exclusively yours as your relationship to Spirit.

Please don't be discouraged if you are not able to sit perfectly still and quiet. It is a huge challenge for me to be still, but when I can carve out any amount of time to try, I always walk away feeling better. I choose not to beat myself up. That's the beauty of thought: you always have choices. Next…

• **Get Quiet** – place yourself in surroundings that are soothing and hold special meaning to you.

• **Take Inventory** – Identify the one issue that is the loudest; one issue that keeps you awake at night or follows you throughout your day. Gently release the others. Imagine you are packing them away on a shelf or tying them to a balloon that is carrying them far away for now. Don't worry, they will return – you are not ignoring them forever.

• **Drop Inside** – Simply ask yourself what wants to be revealed with regard to the issue you identified – what does it want to say to you? Allow yourself not to censor what you are feeling and thinking.

• **Become the Observer** – Allow yourself to "sit with" the feeling/thought. Be mindful of how it shows up in your actions/behaviors. Just watch, do not become overwhelmed with the thought. You are merely an observer.

• **Practice Acceptance** – Allow whatever is there to be there; treat it as if it were your friend (because it is). When we judge or avoid what IS, we create more of the same. Allow whatever is presenting itself to simple be. Talk to the feeling like you would your best friend. Be understanding and accepting of what you are feeling. No running. No excuses. Just accept and allow.

After you experience the shift (it doesn't feel so heavy) ask what your next course of action should be. Be mindful to truly surrender to the process. This inner voice will never cause panic or make you feel afraid. If those feelings come in simply ask them to leave. Breathe through it and shift them out.

JOURNAL

CHAPTER 6

Food, Food and More Food

Our thoughts are powerful. And what do we spend a lot of our time thinking about? Food! But how can we help it? It seems we're constantly being prodded in that direction. Turn on the TV, go to the mall, open a magazine and you are instantly inundated with images and messages, and in some cases, smells. Eat this, it's delicious! You'll love it. This will make you feel better. An evening out always consists of drinks and dinner or grabbing a late-night cappuccino.

Don't forget that childhood rewards revolved around ice cream, pizza and candy. When you were sick, mom made chicken soup to help you feel better. Food is the mortar that binds the building blocks of our lives.

This phenomenon continues well into adulthood. Consider the sample lady in the grocery store who displays a beautifully arranged tray of delicious brownies. You nonchalantly take several swings around her poking through the crowd thinking she won't notice you've been there four times. Or better yet, taking the kids to get one and then using them as an excuse for more.

As you pick up the sample brownie, you think to yourself, "Oh my gosh, no! I can't eat that!" And then follows something along the lines of, "I'm too fat, my butt is too big, and I could barely button these pants this morning." The negative mind chatter continues.

So, let's decode this and consider the messages you send to yourself and out into the universe at the thought/energy level when you talk to yourself in this way:

*"I can't/shouldn't have" = "What I want is bad."
* "I can't have what I want" = "I am not deserving."
* "I'm too fat" = "I am flawed."

And all this occurs over a brownie you didn't even know existed before you entered the store. We allow our thoughts to be influenced and then we accept the negative responses that arise within us.

Is it any wonder that two of the biggest businesses in this country are the food industry and the weight-loss industry? Do you think that is just a coincidence? We're being tied to a yo-yo and we're letting ourselves get bounced back and forth between the two.

Does any of this resonate with your thoughts? Do you feel how you feel when you tell yourself you can't? If you can, you've already taken the first step to changing it.

You don't have to eat those brownies. You don't even have to listen to the sample lady.

It's time to stop the blame cycle and take control of your own thoughts, beliefs, and decisions. How does one do that? Instead of listening to the sample ladies and the marketing strategists, learn to cultivate a relationship with that little voice inside that arises from your Soul. As always, go back to your Soul, trust your gut. But don't confuse your gut with the inner voice that tells you you're fat. There's an easy way to know the difference between the warring voices inside you.

Here's the only guide you need: If that voice tells you something loving, it is Soul. If not, don't listen. We know this kind of thought cycle isn't limited to food.

Reflection

What am I too busy to think about?

_____

What is not thinking about it costing me?

_____

What physical activity would I enjoy doing this week?

_____

What do I want to enjoy this season that I have not made time for?

_____

I tolerate _____ and it makes me feel _____.
Describe the physical feeling of the word you used. How is it showing up physically?

_____

What are three ways I can flow with my life today?

_____

Am I emotionally clogged? What emotional release do I need?

_____

_____

_____

JOURNAL

CHAPTER 7

THE

Weight WAIT

195

125

105

170

110

205

Those of us who have ever lost weight probably agree that losing it was easier than keeping it off. At least I know that is true for me. It seemed almost effortless once I made up my mind to do it; that is, once I thought differently. In fact, I actually became obsessed with my weight loss. Every time my weight loss program leader weighed me, I would hold my breath and wait for her to report the number on the scale before I decided how I was feeling.

As I sadly approached that ominous scale, a perky, size two, recovered "chub-aholic" chirped, "How are you today?"

My canned answer was, "You tell me." Can you begin to see how toxic your thoughts can be? Stress, worry, scarcity, deprivation. All they do is unnecessarily pressure us.

Thoughts create your reality, so the way you think about your body creates it. The Law of Attraction appears again: what you think is what you get. If you are trapped by Madison Avenue's contradicting message that you should eat absolutely everything and weigh absolutely nothing, joyous freedom is as simple as changing the way you think about your body. What if you just decided to love your body unconditionally, right now, the way it is?

I am asking you to entertain the possibility that you seriously need to prepare and invest the energy of time, care and thought to body image, self-esteem and weight acceptance.

In the previous section, I talked about the principle of using Thought-Power and explained how thought can affect our bodies. This is so important I will repeat it: paying attention to your thoughts can allow you to change what were once thought to be pre-existing conditions. Whatever (or whoever) you thought you were, if it is not fully who you dream of being, you can change it, starting now.

When was the last time you spoke to yourself with loving kindness? When was the last time you looked at your naked body in the mirror with total acceptance and love for it? Did you thank it for always being there for you or for literally carrying you?

No matter what a woman really thinks about her weight, she's expected to complain about it to other women. That's what psychology researchers headed by Lauren E. Britton at Appalachian State University in Boone, North Carolina, found in studies of 208 college students. (Morris)
The study proved that when women talk to other women about body image, they instinctively think and share the negative. Imagine what we create with our energy when we do this. Imagine further what we can create if we bend our energy in a positive direction.

I personally have spent a lot of time trying to be prettier. I cried because I didn't have the right nose, and because my cheeks were too fat. At some point I started to wonder who decided that my body was wrong, and I realized was, the answer was me. Only I get to say what works for me and what doesn't. It took years for me to come to that revelation, but I am happy to say I turned it around. And the peace I found in the process has been well worth the time and effort I took to get here. This, my friends, is one of the key messages and purposes of this book. And trust me; if I can do it, you can too.

There is indeed a certain untouchable, uninterrupted peace that comes with leading a life guided by your Soul. Perhaps it's the realization of the impending end, or the ultimate realization: that it's all just beginning and there truly is no ending.

Exercise

The next time you are brushing your teeth, washing your face, or putting on makeup in the bathroom mirror, step back. Look yourself in the eyes. Pay attention to the woman looking back at you. Notice and appreciate her physical features, the wisdom in her eyes, and the kindness in her smile. Smile back, and tell her from your Soul, "I love you."

Self-Talk About Your Body

How do I want to talk to myself?

_____

Is there a voice I'm listening to that doesn't have my best interest at heart?

_____

How do I want to care for myself today? What do I need? How can I gift myself with that?

_____

What would make my body feel loved this week? Get quiet and ask your body what it needs from you.

_____

Today I am grateful for...

_____

_____

JOURNAL

CHAPTER 8

My own story:

From

Whining

to

WINNING

So often we spend our days reliving what we already know. I was living that life until one day I woke up and saw the end. Not the end of my life, but the end of my fear of life, my fear of really living. That's how I know, with every aspect of my being, that this type of transformation is possible for anyone.

My own life story has involved a series of ever-changing definitions. I can remember shopping trips to Macy's with my friend Mary Anne. One day, we spent hours modeling hats for each other and laughing. I felt like Cinderella, trying with all my heart and Soul to find the perfect fit. All I needed was that one hat that complimented my skin tone, my face shape and my personality. And, of course, I'd pray for it to be on sale so I could justify the purchase. After sharing many giggles and tears of happiness with Mary Anne, I finally found the hat that defined me. It accentuated my style, my mood, my body shape and even my status in the world. The hat was perfect except for one snag. It was not on sale. The perfect hat came with a price tag too big to justify, and too hard to swallow. I reluctantly put it back on the rack, fearing the expense of ownership. Quite often that was how I was living my life. Holding back, not taking what I wanted or earned. I lived in fear.

One moment we are confident and certain – sometimes overly certain – about who we are. And then in just a drop of a word, our whole sense of self is open for definition. For example, I get a new hair cut and I'm happy until somebody says, "Ew." I was good with it and became crippled at the hint of judgment from another. Defining ourselves should be something we do as a basic human function with the guidance of a Higher Being. However, most times we allow our mothers-in-law, our friends or our coworkers to define us. Worse yet, we sometimes allow a car or a house or – thank you Verizon – a cell phone to define us. We become what we have and who surrounds us. Sometimes we even become those dead-end, lack-luster jobs we hold. But in order to keep the definition of who we are, we have to have a paycheck to support our position in the world, a position often created from a false reality.

Suddenly, we find ourselves looking for approval from a saleswoman or from other shoppers. We become influenced by outside forces which only make us more confused and scared. The perfect hat suddenly becomes secondary. We focus on all the outside reasons for the hat. Internally we are shattered and uncertain.

Our lives sometimes mirror that trip to the hat department; at least I know mine does. I've been trying hats on for more than 20 years in an effort to reinvent myself over and over. I have tried new hair styles, trendy clothing, stylish handbags, and designer shoes, only to feel more lost and confused with every metamorphosis. I claimed I wanted to embrace change. I whined to all who would listen, even to myself. Of course, my Self was on to me. It recognized my hollow words for what they were. There were no actions attached to them. My Self knew me too well, but I never knew my Self.

I cried and carried on about how true change was too hard. I was afraid. It seemed I was always entering a journey reluctantly, half-heartedly. Typically, I went kicking and screaming, ultimately fighting the next level of personal growth. Nobody likes change. In my heart I knew that embracing my Self would bring me to the next level of my spiritual evolution. I feared growing out of my comfort zone. I told myself I was authentic, but to be authentic I needed to let go of Ego and begin living from my Soul. The eternal question returned: Was I ready? The pain and the fear paralyzed me, and self-inflicted paralysis is the worst kind. I was always wondering if I would ever complete the journey and actually live my life. It was the worst kind of disease: self-defeat.

After lots of sleepless nights and years of therapy my life was transparent, or so I thought. I could finally say that after years of hiding a terrible secret. The secret, no not the affair, the bigger secret that was so shameful I had lost many a night's sleep. Keeping this secret made me feel so lonely and so isolated that I thought death was the only answer.

The secret was that **I had no clue who the hell I was, let alone why I was here.** I couldn't identify any purpose for being on this earth. I hid behind titles, roles and material things. I played what I perceived to be big girl games; games that hurt, embarrassed, and alienated people. Games that bruised people I loved and that pushed myself out of my family members' lives. I was too scared to admit my secret. I spent years blaming everyone for my unhappiness and mistakes. I spent myself into the poorhouse and dragged my family with me. I lived on a diet of credit cards and narcissism.

I began boring myself. I lived to see if I could top myself. I added more drama, more casualties, more angst and more self-loathing. For how long could one person say she was sorry and continue to be self-destructive? For me, it was about eight years. If you didn't look too closely, I was functioning. To the outside world, it looked as if my life was working.

I had a great job, made really good money, a husband who worshipped me and two healthy, outgoing boys. However, on the inside there was a disease that was slowly eating away at my Soul, the very essence of who the Creator sent me here to be.

Slowly, I began to grow up. I realized that if I were truly going to fulfill any kind of bigger purpose something would have to give. And with that, I asked for God to take over.
I promise you I was, and still am, a very ordinary woman who has no special powers. I am simply one who wants to be a better human being. With that thought in mind, I turned inward. I began the tedious task of digging through all the junk that I used as excuses. I spent twelve years in therapy, bought every self-help book known to mankind and began to live a rather self-righteous life. But I was still blaming other people. I developed the ability to be indignant and used God's laws as a shield. Talk about being a bitch. Here I was rehabbed, reformed and ready to fix your ass.

And fix it I would. If you didn't agree with me, I cut you off. If you challenged me with questions I didn't like, I said adios. You were dead to me if you didn't fall in line with my values and my principles. Nice, right? But I was still hiding and still feeling disconnected.

Although I was closer to the truth than I ever had been, I needed the other shoe to drop, and boy, did it drop. Just when I thought I was on the road to knowing who I was and what I wanted, indiscretions began to haunt me. All the images of this self-deprecating affair resurfaced, over and over, and over again. OH NO! Could I have grown a conscience? There is a literal rock bottom. It's different for all of us and only we can define it for ourselves. But our greatest moment as human beings is when we hear that resounding "THUD." Contrary to popular belief, hitting the bottom has a way of opening our eyes.

I began to feel the pain of knowing I had crossed the line between right and wrong. Painful memories vividly reappeared. Fast forward. I climbed up from the bottom using faith, humility, patience, hope, God, family, and friends as a ladder. My climb was arduous and filled with remorse. Remember, no one ever said it would be easy. I promise you though, it was worth it.

One happy result is that I vowed to use my life as a resource. The open book of my life is available as a "how to" for your journey to the deepest part of un-forgiveness. I shine the light by asking questions that are too tough for you to ask yourself. I don't allow the bullshit to build up, I don't blow smoke, and I have no stomach for victim mentality. I allow it to show up and be acknowledged, but it's not welcome and it certainly cannot stay.

One morning as I stared at my forty-year-old face in the mirror and soaked in every pore, every line, and every stray hair, I accepted the inevitable. As we age, our looks are basically the same. Everything just gets longer and more jiggly. The once firm, supple breasts hang shapelessly, yesterday's taut chin swings frantically with each hearty laugh. And of course, there's the never-ending ripple effect produced as we fan our bodies gripped by hot flashes. The truth is we are all getting older. The good news is that from a Soul perspective, there is no such thing as aging.

My journey to self-acceptance began later that same morning in my car. Having overslept, I was frantically driving to work, checking my makeup at the same time. At a stop light I pulled down my visor, opened the mirror and took a long, close look at the face staring back at me. At first I was shocked to see myself wearing sheet marks that had not been washed away in the shower, soothed by the moisturizer, or rubbed away by the foundation I had applied. After several seconds of confusion and numerous honking horns, I horrifically realized these were not sheet marks. These were hash marks that tallied up throughout my life. In them I saw all the bridges burned, loves lost, enemies made, and friends earned. I was wearing my life on my face for the entire world to see. I suddenly caught a glimpse of the scared little girl from the 70s, the new mom of the 80s, the career woman and adulteress of the 90s, and finally the mature, spiritually grounded, content woman of the new millennium.

In that moment I realized there was so much more to experience. I needed to find a way to embrace my face, not Estee Lauder's or Christian Dior's or Mary Kay's, but my face with all its glorious imperfections. As clichéd as it sounds, I needed to love myself. All those revelations occurred in the time it took the traffic light to change from red to green.

Have you ever had the feeling that your insides are slowly seeping out through your pores? It's a sensation that begs for attention. It gnaws at our center and sometimes even urgently rumbles our intestines. If we're lucky, every once in a while we experience something that creates that very feeling in us. That is the feeling of surrender, of letting go, of self-growth.

Surrendering to Spirit saved me, but I had help from my ability to laugh at myself, at my situations, at my behavior, and at my mistakes. The biggest laugh of all came when I realized that all along I had the power to change course, and chart new territories. All I had to do was be aware enough to seek different avenues.

I am amazed that the journey of my life so far – a seeming eternity – has been a mere blip on the radar in the entire scheme of things. I very consciously choose to savor every single experience and not to label it. I know in my heart there is no right or wrong, good or bad, there *just* is. I have let all expectations go. Intuition and free will guide me. So far I am having a blast. Every day is a new joy and every experience is filled with love. Not bad for a recovered narcissist.

JOURNAL

CHAPTER 9

SOUL VISION

-Life Mission

So often we go about living our lives in a bubble, a protected environment that is nevertheless subject to change by society's expectations. We are slaves to conformity until the day we can no longer deny we are living a joyless existence. One day we wake up to our Soul screaming for attention. It screams so loudly others around us can often hear it in our interactions and reactions. We play the victim, lash out at others, gossip.

We look different to everyone around us. We are misaligned and suffering. We are constantly creating drama and fighting with reality.

Inevitably, something happens that forces us to get quiet and look at our authentic selves.

I've identified the four D's that typically call us to look within: Disease, Death, Divorce, and Disaster. When one or more of these occur, our lives break open. Everything around us falls apart. Finally realizing we have nowhere to turn but inward, we surrender. It's a blessed portal to the next phase of the journey. It's when we decide it's easier to live authentically, once our personal authenticity is clearly defined.

As we fight our way through the confusion and chaos, we need to keep our eye on the vision that resides within our Soul, our Life's Purpose. We have been trained to avoid chaos, and our mentality is to avoid irritation in order to create and follow our bliss. But pay attention to the irritant, that sand in the oyster that is the beginning of the true path to spiritual growth. That itch, that irritation is what launches the learning. The next time you are irked, I encourage you to take a breath, step out of yourself, and observe. Examine

the situation from an outside perspective and indentify the growth opportunity. I promise you there will be one.

Reflection

What one thing will I do today to feed my Life's Purpose?

_____

What am I most passionate about this week? What attracts my attention?

_____

What does my Soul desire this week?

_____

What do I want to say "No" to this week? What is it that will drain my energy if I don't set boundaries and practice saying no?

_____

What do I want to give myself permission to do? What makes me joyous?

_____

What nurtures and calms my Soul? Explore your Soul.

_____

This week I trust…

_____

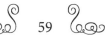

JOURNAL

CHAPTER 10

BUBBLE
WRAP

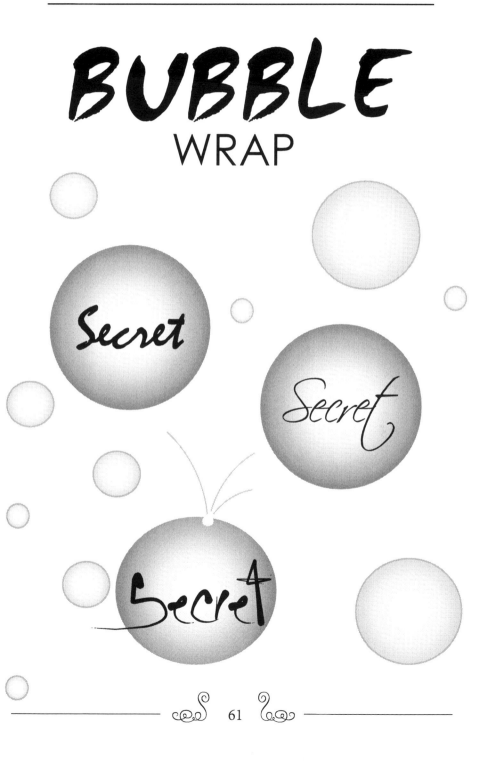

Bubble wrap is a pliable transparent plastic material commonly used for packing fragile items. Regularly spaced, protruding, air-filled hemispheres – bubbles – provide cushioning for precious or breakable items. Who hasn't received a package secured and protected by bubble wrap?

So often we walk around keeping a secret that is gently wrapped in bubble wrap, believing in the fragility of Self. It's not an earth-shattering secret, although we think it is. The 12th-century Persian poet Rumi speaks of the Open Secret. He says that each one of us is trying to hide a secret – not a big secret – but a more subtle and pervasive one. It's the secret that you and I keep from each other every day.

Have you ever run into someone only to exaggerate how wonderful your life is when in reality it's slowly crumbling around you with every breath you take? We are so busy worrying about what others think or have that we feel the need to hide ourselves or wrap ourselves in bubble wrap as a form of shallow self-protection.

The truth about our humanity is that our secret is not really a secret at all. How can it be when we're all protecting the very same story? That's why Rumi calls it an Open Secret. Each one of us protects it.

Rumi tells us that the moment we accept the troubles we've been given, the door will open. It sounds easy and attractive, but it is difficult and most of us pound on the door to freedom and happiness with every manipulative ploy we can conjure up, and save the one that actually works.

If you're interested in opening this door to heavenly fortunes, start with the door to your own secret Self; your Soul. See what happens when you peer into who you really are. Start slowly. Without getting dramatic, share the simple dignity of yourself in each moment: triumphs and failures, satisfaction and sorrow.

Face your embarrassment at being human and you'll uncover a deep well of passion and compassion. It's a great power, your Open Secret. When your heart is unshielded you make it safe for whomever you meet to put down his burden of hiding so both of you can walk through the open door. Discuss who you are at your core. If you squeeze an orange, juice comes out; but what comes out when it is you that is being squeezed or pressured? Who are you at your core at a Soul level? How can you work at knowing, changing, or living your core? The answer is still conscious awareness.

Similar to bubble wrap is that protective wall of self-doubt that we build around ourselves.

We'll only go so far in accepting and giving love. Our fear of rejection and our lack of self-esteem cripple us from plowing forward and really living from our Soul. Our focus is not necessarily on why the wall exists, but rather how to dismantle it.

I am an advocate of psychological therapy, though I feel that this is purely a personal choice. Therapy to me is like an archeological dig where the therapist is the chief archeologist. The therapist leads us to the burial ground, but it's our job to unearth what's beneath the surface. As a coach, however, I focus on destiny and willingness to put the walls aside regardless of the reason they exist. Allow yourself to think for one moment who you would be without your walls. Take a few moments in quiet meditation and capture a glimpse just beyond the walls. What do you see? Ask yourself, who would you be without the walls? What gifts would you bring to the world and to yourself?

Reflection

I am ready to receive

_____

How is confusion showing up in my life?

_____

What gifts are wrapped in the confusion?

_____

Am I willing to look for them? Get silent and ask Source for guidance.

_____

What am I feeling at this moment in my life?

_____

What does this feeling really mean? How can I dismantle this fear?

_____

_____

Am I emotionally clogged? What emotional release do I need?

_____

_____

Get quiet and communicate with your body. What messages is it sending you? What does it need from you? Remember your body is home to your Soul.

_____

_____

_____

_____

When I am feeling emotionally and physically drained these days, what feeling am I experiencing? What is the root cause?

_____

_____

_____

_____

Today I am grateful for...

_____

_____

_____

_____

_____

JOURNAL

CHAPTER 11

UNLOCK THE
treasures
WITHIN

Meet Sandy

Most times if are willing to look within we can very clearly see the story we are living. Our quiet calls of desperation that we muffle as we smile through our teeth and answer "I'm fine" to the question, "How are you doing?"

This is the story of "Sandy", a lonely woman who discarded her dignity to find her happiness.

Sandy grew up lower middle class with a heavy a stigma attached to her regarding self worth. She constantly looked for Mr. "I Do" from the minute she graduated high school. She was programmed to believe she would never find him. So, she settled for Mr. "You'll Do." She turned a lot of rocks over to find the men she was attracting. Sandy used her sexuality to begin relationships. The decade of the 80's introduced us to technology that enabled us to meet people from around the globe. It opened up a whole new way to flirt, date and even find true love. Sandy was no exception; in fact she found her stride during the instant messaging era. Now she could find men who would understand her, be compassionate and listen, if only to her typed words. She longed for the intimate bond that she believed would define her.

Sandy was a wonderful woman with a gigantic heart. She was funny, personable, and successful and longed for Mr. "I Do". He was at the center of everything Sandy did. Everywhere she went she was scoping out potential mates. With the advent of instant messaging, a whole new world literally opened for her. She was "meeting" men constantly, both literally and figuratively. It became common practice for her pack up on the weekends and head off to meet her newest "love" face to face. Throwing all caution to the wind, she ventured out into the big world of possibilities. She was dating more than ever but was further from happy than she'd ever been.

After countless one night stands and numerous supposedly monogamous relationships, she finally got her wake up call. She had arranged to go out of town and meet a man she had been instant messaging with for several months. He seemed nice enough and she felt chemistry if only via a computer screen. Off she went. She arrived at the hotel hours before he did. She primped and prettied, you know all the routine things we do when we are infatuated. Soon, there was knock at the door and there he was in the flesh. Not only was he there but he brought a friend. WHAT, A FRIEND? Yes, a friend. He understood how much Sandy loved sex and how open she was to exploring, so he brought a buddy to join in their special night. Sandy followed through with a night of sexcapades and later admitted she was sickened by what had transpired, but that she felt like there was no way out; after all, maybe he really loved her.

Sandy's story is extreme, but is reflective of the energy women put out when looking for Mr. "I Do". Take a few moments and look quietly within. Take time to identify your essence energy. How are you portraying yourself? Is your true essence aligning with what you want to attract? If not, how can you make the shift?

Unfortunately it's common practice to look outside of ourselves for answers. <u>For some reason we trust other people to know what's best for us.</u> **Reread those words.**

What is your "Sandy" story?

If you are willing to look within, you will see the strength of Soul. The Spirit within is no match for the fragility of the Ego, yet many of us live from the ego for fear that touching the Soul will break us. Ego is that conditioned voice inside of us that likes to keep us stuck and dependent on outside sources for comfort and value. Soul, on the other hand, is that gentle, quiet, peaceful place that never fights our thoughts in a way that is harmful to us. We have become conditioned to believe that in order for something to be valuable or useful we must sweat and break the bank to get it. Not so. If you take nothing more from this book, please take the fact that living from your core, your Soul, is the simplest thing you can ever do. It's natural. Just as birds fly and dogs bark, living from our Souls is encoded within us. It's the outside programming that isn't natural.

The process of "allowing" has a natural ease to it. It allows us to just be. That's what it means to live from Soul. As we effortlessly float through life on wings as light as air, we're always looking for seeds to plant. Planting the seeds and allowing the process to unfold naturally is about as close to the Source, God, or Divine that one can get. Consider the development of life in the womb. The process is destined and facilitated by the Divine. It takes little or no effort for humankind to nurture and grow life, or to fortify our spiritual muscle. Similarly, allowing our spiritual muscle to build connects us to our Source, our Soul.

I will ask again: What's inside of who you are? Do you love what comes out, or do your struggle to keep it hidden? Do you even realize what comes out? Where does the awareness process start? You must first turn inward and remove the bubble wrap.

Allow access for the gentle possibilities that await you. Live in bewilderment with childlike wonder. Become curious, and explore. Open yourself up and know that you are protected by something much bigger than you are. Eleanor Roosevelt said it best: "Do one thing every day that scares you."

Reflection

What possibilities are you willing to acknowledge?

_____

_____

Explore what you are willing to do today to live outside the box.

_____

_____

If I had no fears what one thing would I like to accomplish in my lifetime?

_____

_____

What love and attention would you love to give yourself this week?

_____

If I knew that this week was the last week I'd have here on earth, what would I choose to do with my precious energy this week?

_____

_____

What wisdom can I call up from the generations of women I've known to help me radiate love and gratitude to the world?

_____

_____

What small, sweet steps can I take that will simplify my routine, as well as let me experience the grace of ease?

_____

_____

How can I best honor my relationship with the Source of all life?

_____

_____

_____

What gifts do I possess that I have kept hidden?

_____

_____

What am I willing to take responsibility for today that I have been blaming someone else for?

_____

_____

_____

JOURNAL

CHAPTER 12

JUST

Like a child clings to its mother, we cling to our Creator, the Source that feeds us. It is a gift to bathe in the glory that is the Love of the One.

We are created in the image of our Source, and we must be what we came from, so why is it that so many of us refuse to value ourselves and our worth? Too often we smile the smile, exchange the greetings and then revert to a blanket of self doubt, fear and insecurity. How do we begin the journey the Creator? Is it a journey best taken with a friend, in solitude, or with the Creator? What works best for you?

There are is no right or wrong way to make this journey. There's no peril involved such as finding yourself way off course after making one simple wrong turn. The journey, as I see it, is about knowing that exactly where you are is exactly where you belong. There's no big mystery involving directions, carpooling or worshipping. You're there.

To "be" implies a moving, dynamic fluidity, ever evolving, ever growing. We run from day to day, month to month, year to year without ever stopping simply to "be". We say we are "being," but when we say it, do we attach another word to it? If we are being calm, being reflective or being joyous are we ever truly just being?

Being involves stillness and silence. No movement either in body or mind. I know it sounds powerful, scary and nearly impossible. The concept itself is what throws us off center, shakes our core and makes our minds race. Is it the introduction to the Soul that terrifies us? If we can just be in the moment then we will have no excuses, no interruptions and no choice but to see who we are.

The very fear of really knowing who we are causes internal and external struggles. Instead of facing who we are head on, we wage wars that bring nations to ruins, we feed addictions and we dodge happiness more than ever. However, if we begin to eliminate the fear of looking within we know exactly what we are dealing with and that empowers us to make choices to support our highest and greatest good.

The grace that flows from being reveals itself in the smile of strangers, the helping hand of volunteers, and at food banks and homeless shelters. At some point being enters the life of each individual who serves others. Service to others is the cornerstone to being. Service is born from gratitude for all that simply is. When we are grateful, we realize that life is bigger than just who we are or what we need. By bathing in the light of our Source we will experience being through gratitude. If only for today, just be.

JOURNAL

CHAPTER 13

My *Wish* for You

Fast Forward…

Today finds me living in the moment. Savoring all the inner peace and love that comes from knowing myself at a Soul level and dedicating my life to God.

I am certain that if I was able to make this journey, anyone can. It takes a willingness to wake up to what IS, and a radical acceptance of it.

I remember my very first psychotherapy appointment. The therapist asked me "What do you want the outcome to be from our sessions?" My answer was "inner peace". Little did I know it would be more than a decade later and with a self-propelled search before I would finally look back on all the years of my life and feel at peace.

After reading this book, I hope that you were inspired to be curious enough to explore. The beauty of the Soul shines so brightly that it illuminates the way for everything else to fall into place. If only for today, I encourage you to fall in love with yourself. Be at peace with yourself and the world around you. Become one with the Spirit within.

JOURNAL

PART 2

THE GIFT OF

Journaling

CHAPTER 14

Journaling
FOR THE SOUL

For as long as I can remember I have always loved to doodle words and pictures on paper. It wasn't until I came to live life consciously and on purpose that I realized my own words were my own solutions. When I journal, there is a process, a routine, a ritual. I call on Spirit to help reveal what is in my highest and greatest good.

Most times I am guided to allow the words to simply flow from my pen and only when I reread them do I realize that spirit was writing through me. I simply got out of the way and let my fingers type the words Spirit put into my heart.

The following chapters are more journaling questions to help you on your journey. I have chosen several words that were a huge part of my spiritual evolution in order to share my experience with you. Here are some questions to empower you on your personal journey.

JOURNAL

CHAPTER 15

Forgiveness

Imagine going to the deepest, darkest part of your Soul, a place that holds all the resentments, all the frustrations, all the people to whom you have shown no mercy because in your mind, they wronged you. Picture them as imprisoned in a dark, dank place that haunts you every time you think of it.

This is the place you keep score of every wrong done to you and every person who made it happen. The place is so cluttered you can't even visit it without feeling trapped. Your breathing gets shallow, you begin to sweat with the very idea of seeing this person's face or even hearing his or her voice. This pit is so dark and dismal it manifests in you physically. This is what I call "un-forgiveness". It is your hell and the only person caged and trapped there is you.

I learned a long time ago the only way to release the prisoner, me, was to use the "F" word: Forgiveness. Forgiveness is a powerful word and the power is contained in the thought. You may never even get to speak your forgiveness to a certain person, but simply by thinking it you will free yourself and a free Self is an empowered self. No more victim. You're responsible for the choice.

Remember, you may be holding yourself prisoner by not offering forgiveness to yourself.

In order to begin the process, I encourage you to sit with Spirit and journal. To get you started I offer a few of the questions that guided me. As you journal you may be given more questions by Spirit to reflect on. Open your heart and Soul to this process and feel the freedom.

Experiencing Forgiveness

Who do I need to forgive so that I can release the toxins in my Soul?

_____

_____

_____

What am I willing to forgive myself for?

_____

_____

_____

What burden from the past am I carrying with me? Am I willing to release it? What process can I use to release?

_____

_____

Describe what forgiveness feels like. Use your creative Self to deliver the message.

_____

_____

I give myself permission to…

_____

_____

JOURNAL

CHAPTER 16

DRAMA

Television sells it to us, magazines offer it up in large doses, co-workers serve it up and of course, family members slather it on. In true soap opera fashion I lived at the height of drama. It was the drug of choice throughout my life, and if there wasn't any, I created it. What role did I play? I played the victim, of course. I didn't do anything wrong, I was wronged. Drama was mine to enjoy.

One time an ex-employer had the nerve to tell me I was a drama queen and that everywhere I went drama followed. Imagine how that went: I put his ass right in my un-forgiveness dungeon and there he stayed throughout my employment, which by the way, lasted for five years after his statement. For five years it festered and fermented in the dungeon within me. I reeked of anger, revenge, and "fuck you".

That was the attitude I put on every day to go to work. When I look back I can't even believe I made it through as well as I did. The anger and resentment fueled my search for new employment. Thankfully, Spirit took over and would not allow me to find another job. I was forced to work though the pieces. It was painful, hard and frustrating, but all worth it.

Unraveling the Dramatic Thoughts

What drama am I feeding in my life today, this week, and this month?

_____

_____

_____

Who do I allow in my life that feeds me drama?

_____

_____

How does drama make me feel physically?

_____

_____

What does a drama-free zone look like? Is it an attitude, a space, a set of boundaries?

_____

_____

Explore what a drama-free life looks and feels like.

_____

_____

List the positives and the negatives of having drama.

_____

_____

Is there anyone in my life that brings nothing but drama? If so, am I willing to gently and lovingly release that person from my life?

_____

_____

JOURNAL

CHAPTER 17

TRUST

Trust: *a: assured reliance on the character, ability, strength, or truth of someone or something; b: one in which confidence is placed.* –Merriam-Webster online dictionary

Trust has always been the biggest obstacle for me to conquer. Throughout my entire life I was taught not to trust anyone or anything and to fear everything. "People will get you if _____." "Don't believe what people tell you." And, of course, the continuous broken promises as a child, whether it is "I'll take you to the park," "We're going to the beach," or "I'm your mom and I'll never leave you." These were all stories I grew up on.

After hearing broken promises for so long, you begin to think everyone will break their word.
You even begin to believe that you can't trust yourself to make decisions, choose friends, or select jobs. Your life is built on complete uncertainty. You find yourself doubting people before they even speak. You judge everyone, even yourself, as unreliable.

Breaking that conditioned pattern was the hardest favor I ever did for myself. My entire life had been about looking for the loophole in the story and sleuthing to find the truth because no one ever told it. One day, however, I simply decided that no matter what other people did or didn't do was of no concern to me. I realized by having expectations, I created the perfect environment to be let down and to generate mistrust. I knew I had to just let people be who they were.

Of course, respect needed to be the core of all encounters, whether I was giving or receiving. I started out giving people the option to be themselves and something really amazing happened. My heart opened and I stopped looking for loopholes. Living got a lot easier. After all, I didn't have to spend energy trying to catch people in a lie.

Weave simplicity. Begin with TRUST

Am I trustworthy? Examine different situations in your life that lead you to your answer.

_____

_____

Who do I trust most in my life? What characteristics do they possess?

_____

_____

Which relationship in my life lacks trust? What am I willing to do about it?

_____

_____

Is there someone in my life that I mistrust? Am I willing to release this person from my life?

_____

_____

_____

_____

JOURNAL

CHAPTER 18

Beauty

As I sit here in my forty-ninth year of life, I covet the warm thoughts that arise from my Soul as I think about my beauty. I assure you – and as you read earlier – I wasn't always in a place to be comfortable being me. It was through revolution – world wars within me – and evolution (growth) that I now simply and completely embrace my beauty as a woman.

My beauty has nothing to do with my physicality. My beauty is in my core, in my kindness to a stranger, in my comforting smile to a crying child, in my loving words to a lonely widow or a broken divorcée. Beauty isn't what you look like; it's the energy you reflect.

I encourage you to embrace the beauty in you with renewed vigor and excitement. Begin to notice subtle changes in those around you, but mostly within yourself.

To Be Beauty

What does it mean to feel beautiful?

_____

_____

Describe the last time you felt beautiful. What were you doing? Where were you? Was the beauty internal or external?

_____

_____

_____

Who is the most beautiful woman you know? What makes her beautiful to you?

_____

_____

_____

Take time tomorrow evening and watch the sun set. Use your senses to experience the setting sun. Share your feelings in writing so that you can forever live them.

_____

_____

_____

_____

Take time to think about your beauty. Explore through thoughts and words what is most beautiful about you.

_____

_____

_____

_____

_____

_____

_____

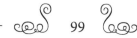

JOURNAL

About the Author

Veronica Drake is an International Relationship Coach. She works with women who are struggling to regain trust and self respect after the break up. She helps them develop their intuitive voice so they can make powerful decisions when designing future relationships.

Veronica's intuitive abilities are amazingly insightful and accurate. Her intuitive gifts empower her clients to journey deep into self-discovery … and create a deeper connection to their own intuitive voice.

She uses her witty, warm and sassy sense of humor to help clients relax, release and get in touch with what really matters to them.

Visit her at www.designyourrelationships.com

This book will take you on a journey to the deepest part of you. You will laugh, cry, and maybe deny, but you will want to embrace the face and body that is YOU. Share in the energy of unconditional love and acceptance contained in this book. It's time to re-learn whatever you think you know about YOU!

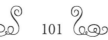

Tired of…

- Attracting Mr. You'll Do instead of Mr. I Do

- Tired of hiding behind the old belief of you're not good enough

- Emotional Vampires sucking the life out of you

- Feeling frustrated

It's time to discover the

 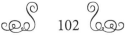

ARTWORK

Cover Designed by:
Hummingbird Creative Concepts
www.hummingbirdcreativeconcepts.com

Book Layout & Design by:
Sarah Johnson
www.sljdesign.com

Made in the USA
Charleston, SC
09 February 2012